COLORING BOOKS
FOR GROWN-UPS

OODLES
of
DOODLES

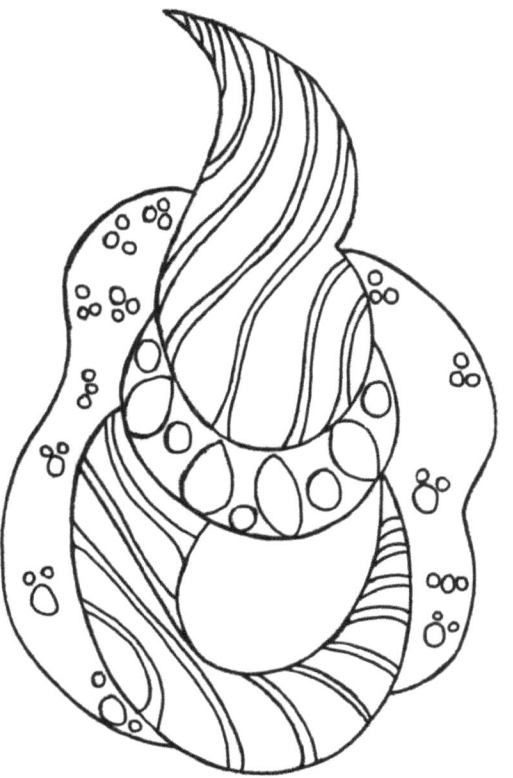

Illustrations by Deanna Pipkin.

ISBN-13: 978-1517014551
ISBN-10: 1517014557

deannasdoodles.webs.com

Wingfeather Books

wingfeatherbooks.com

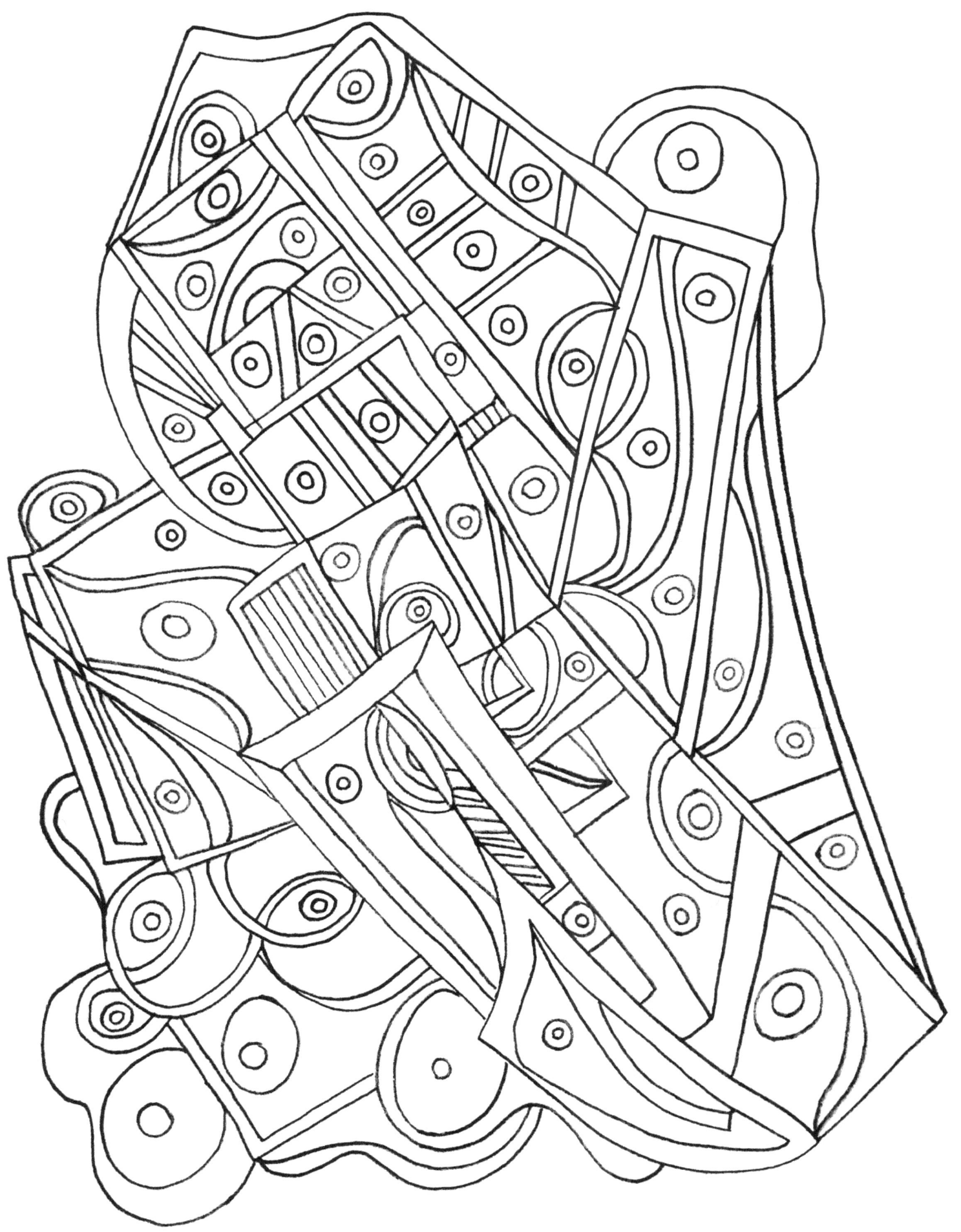

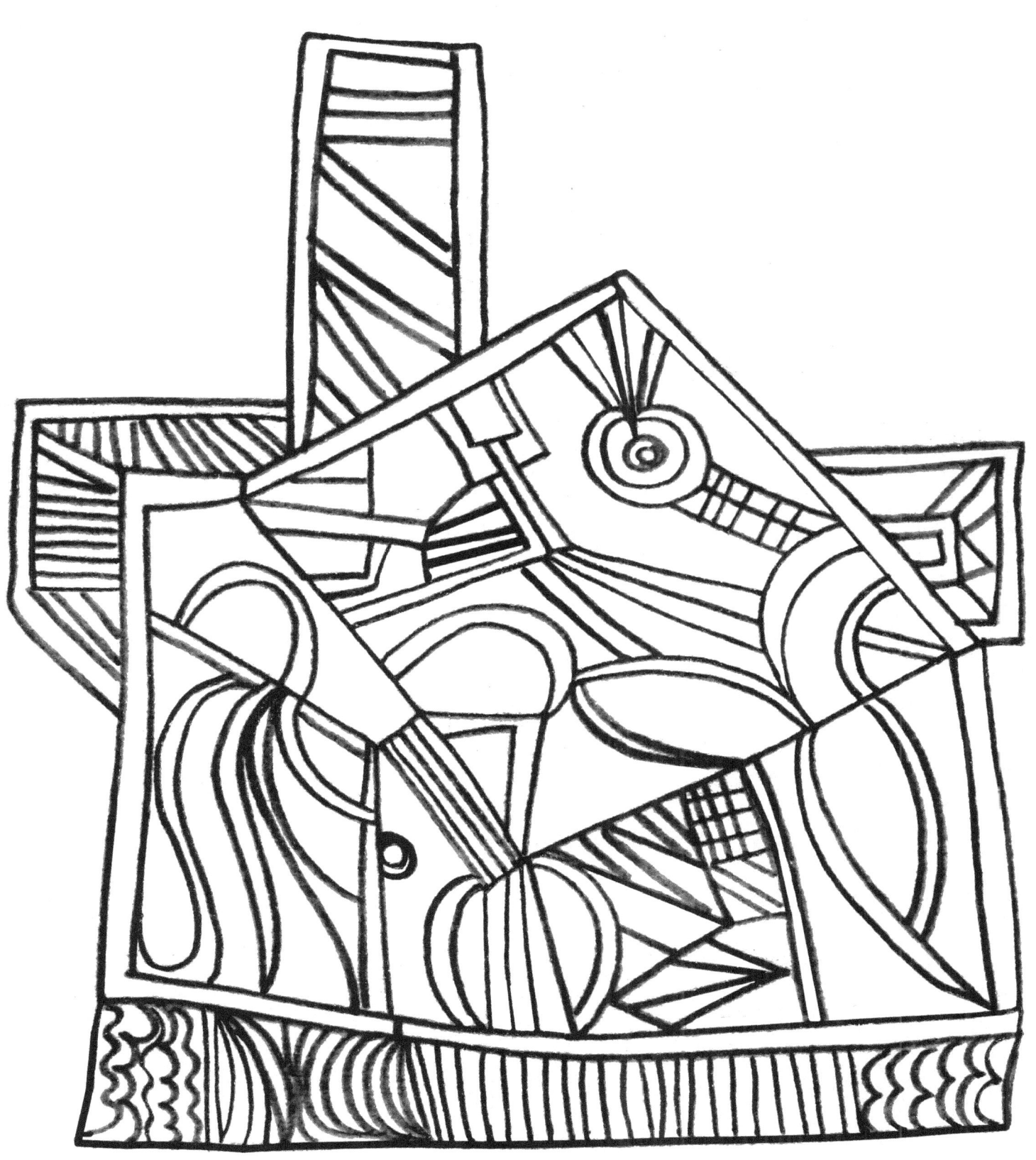

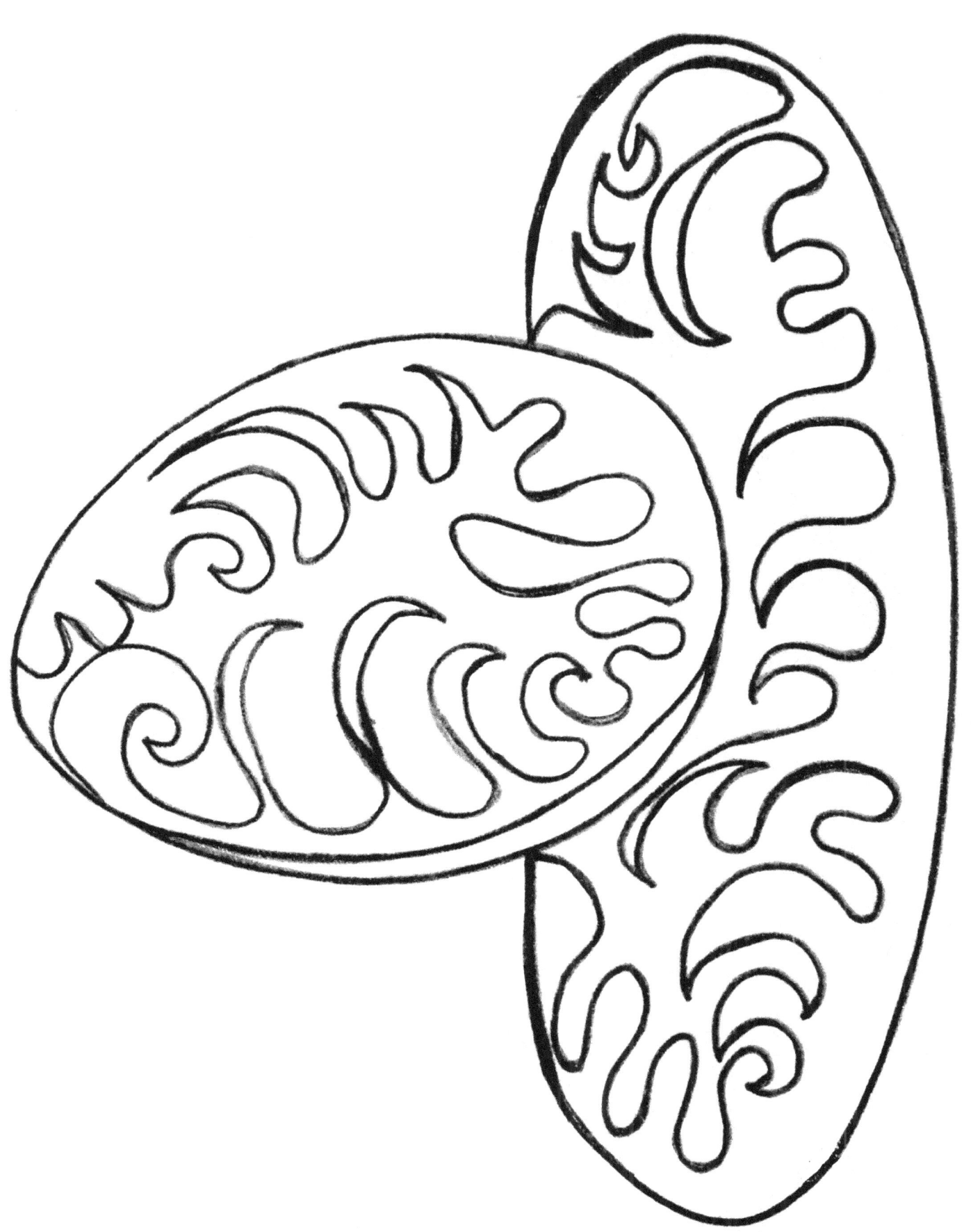

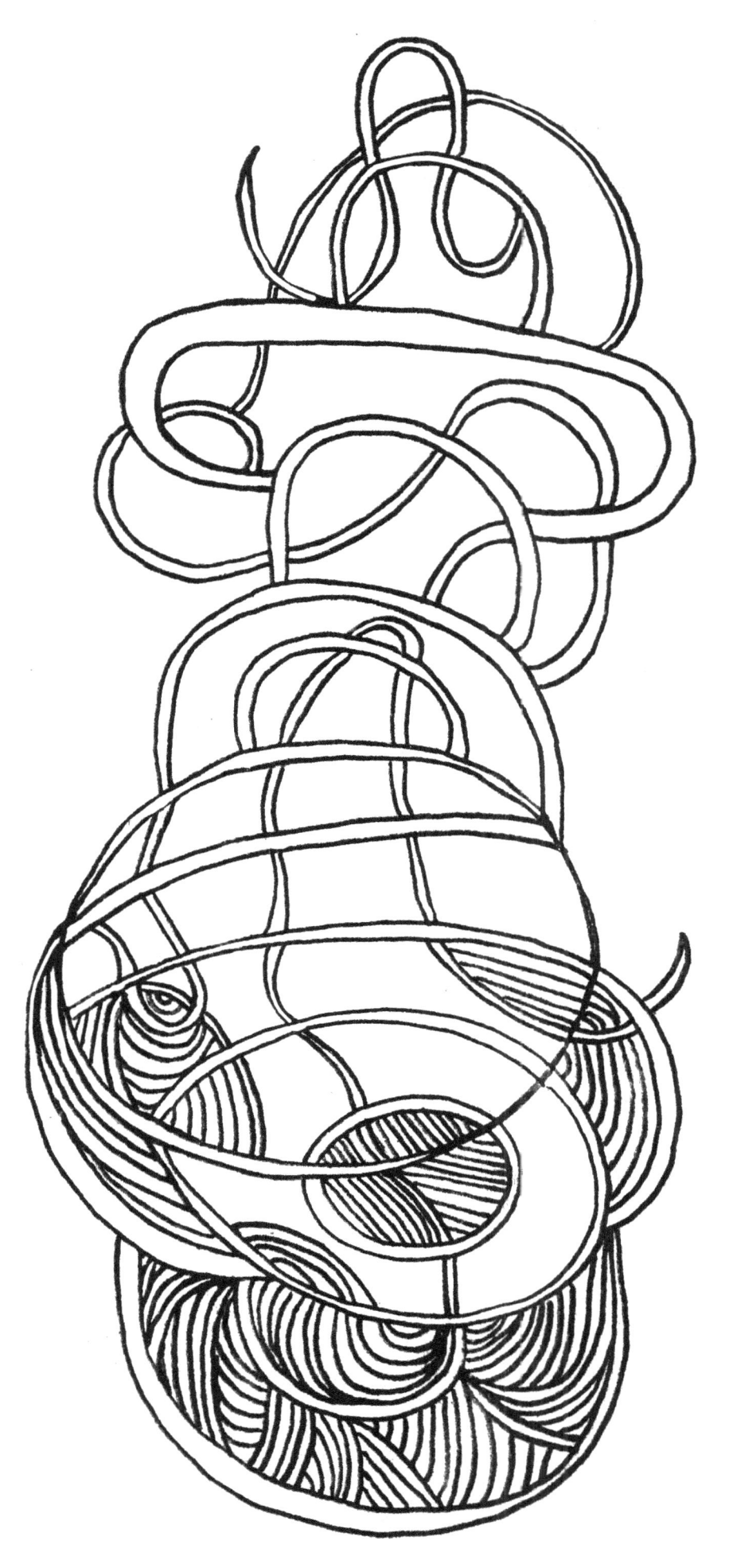

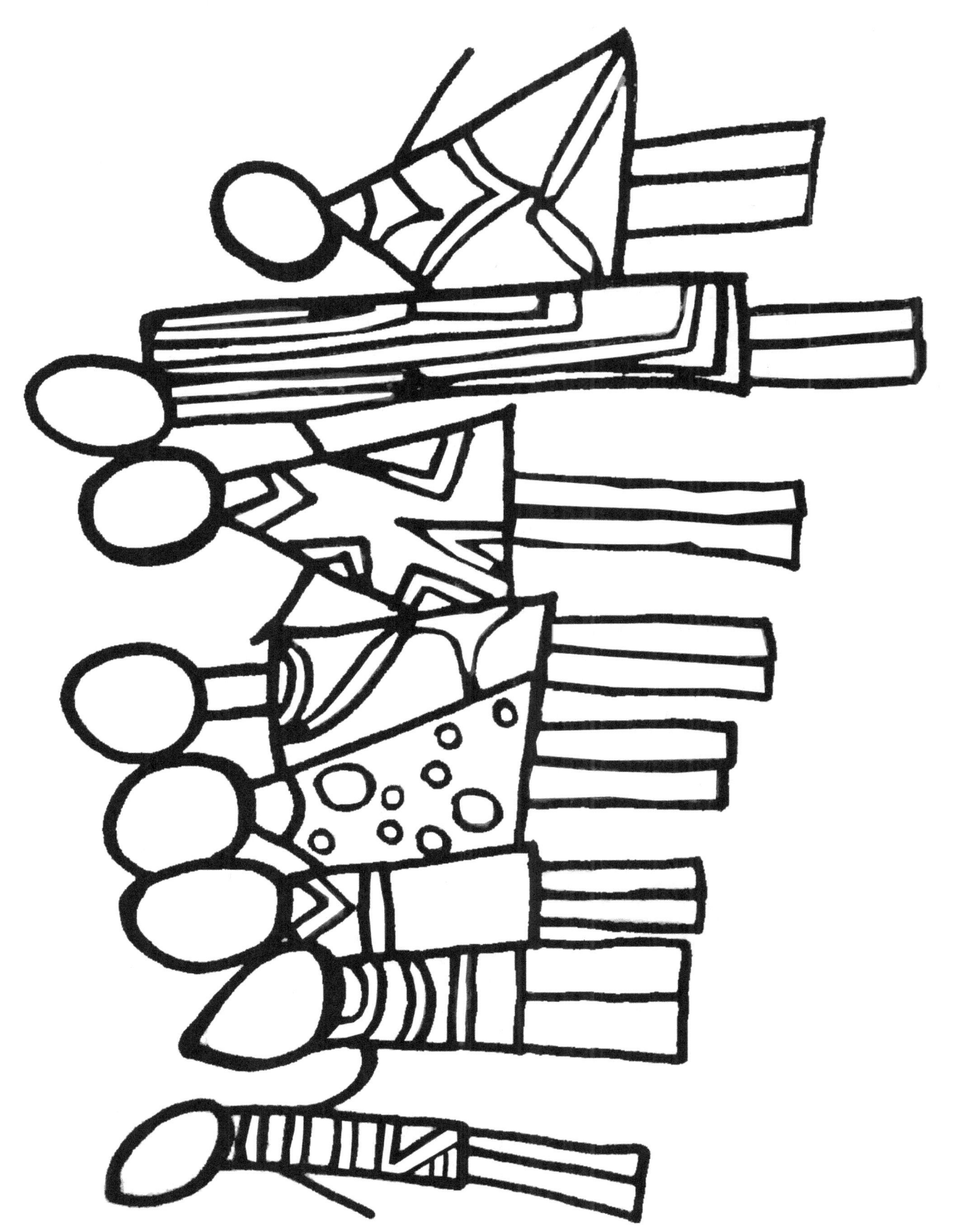

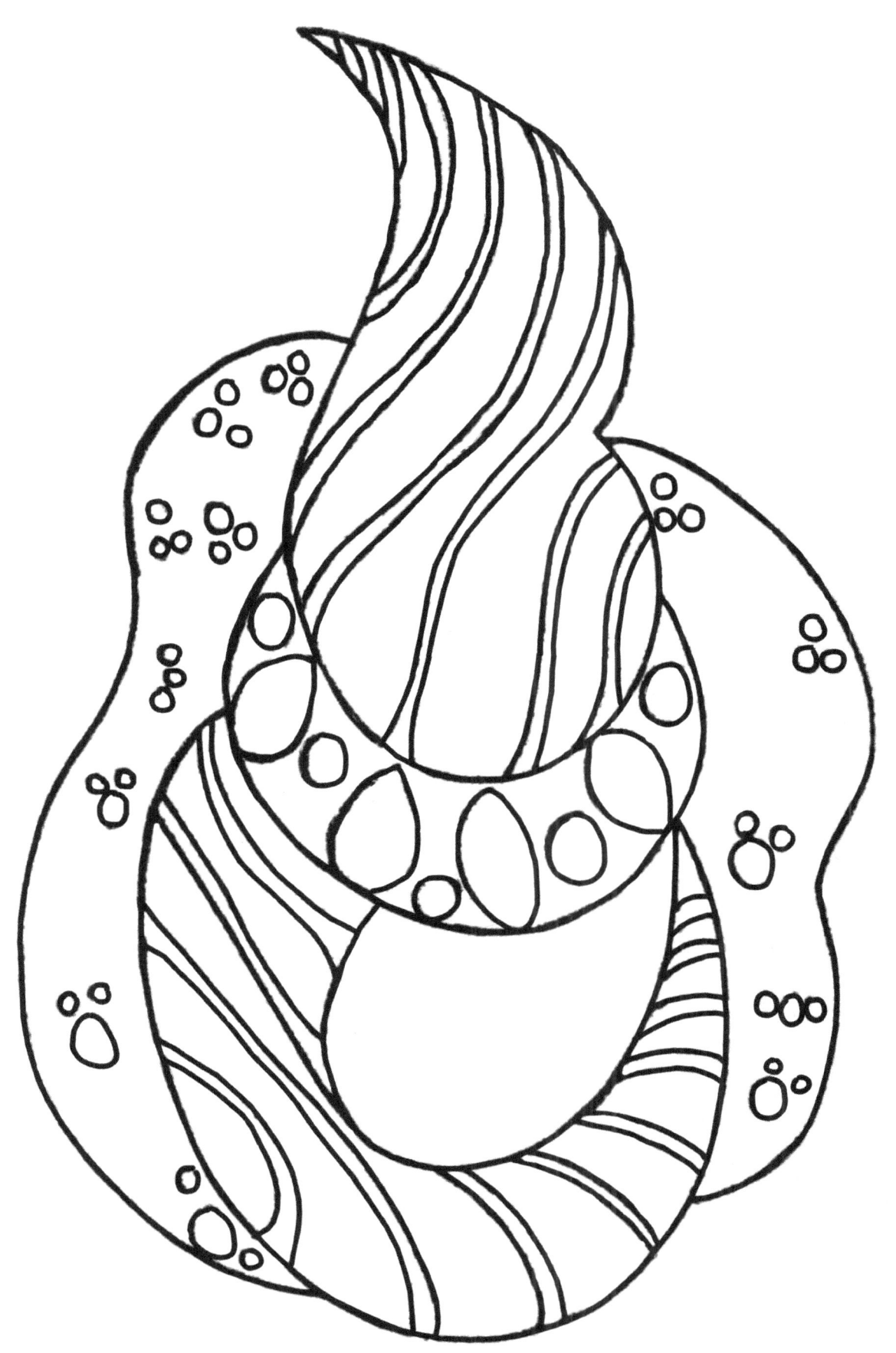

BONUS coloring page from

Grandma's Quilts by Cheryl Casey

Tear out and use
as blotter between
pages if needed

Tear out and use
as blotter between
pages if needed